Curious Questions & Answers about...

Our Oceans

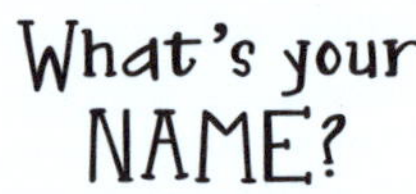

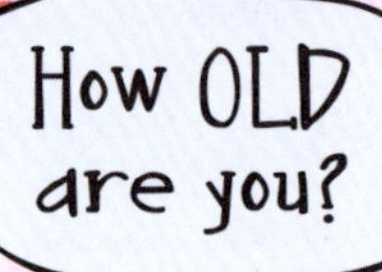

First published in 2019 by Miles Kelly Publishing Ltd
Harding's Barn, Bardfield End Green, Thaxted, Essex, CM6 3PX, UK
Unit 5A The Court, Ashbourne Industrial Estate, Ashbourne,
Co. Meath, A84 DP73, Eire

2 4 6 8 10 9 7 5 3 1

Publishing Director Belinda Gallagher
Creative Director Jo Cowan
Editorial Director Rosie Neave
Design Manager Joe Jones
Cover Designers Andrea Slane, Mark Penfound
Image Manager Liberty Newton
Production Elizabeth Collins
Reprographics Stephan Davis
Assets Venita Kidwai

ISBN 978-1-83515-095-5

Printed in China

British Library Cataloguing-in-Publication Data
A catalogue record for this book is available from the British Library

Made with paper from a sustainable forest

www.mileskelly.net

CURIOUS
QUESTIONS & ANSWERS ABOUT...
Our Oceans

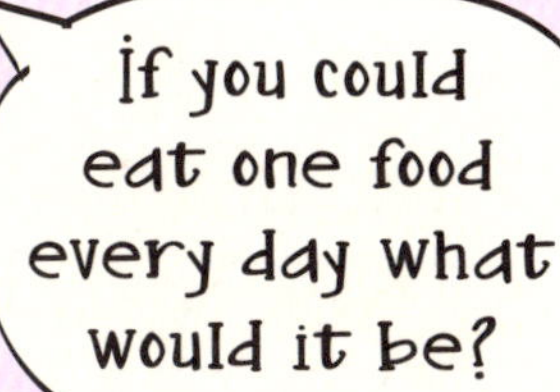

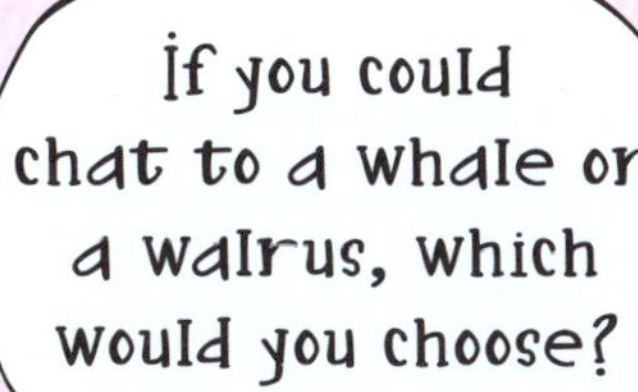

Words by **Camilla de la Bédoyère**

Illustrations by **Tim Budgen**

MILES KELLY

How big is an ocean?

There are five oceans
and they are
all HUGE!
Together, they
cover two thirds
of Earth's surface.

Day octopus

Long-snouted seahorse

Are the oceans important?

Yes, billions of animals and plants live in them!
People use the things that live in the ocean
for all sorts of things, too. A type of seaweed
called red algae is used in peanut butter –
it makes it easy to spread!

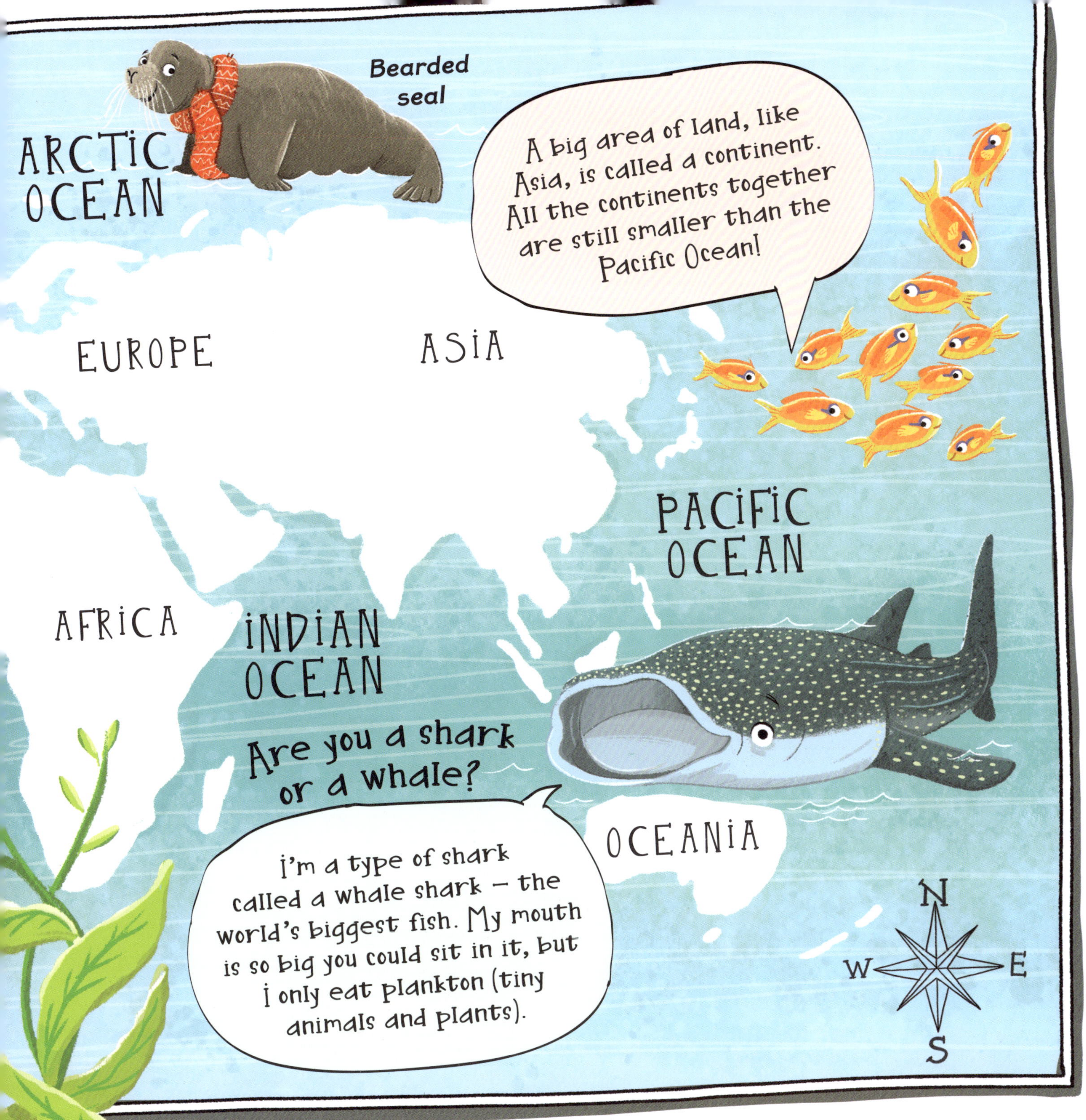

ARCTIC OCEAN

Why is the sea blue?

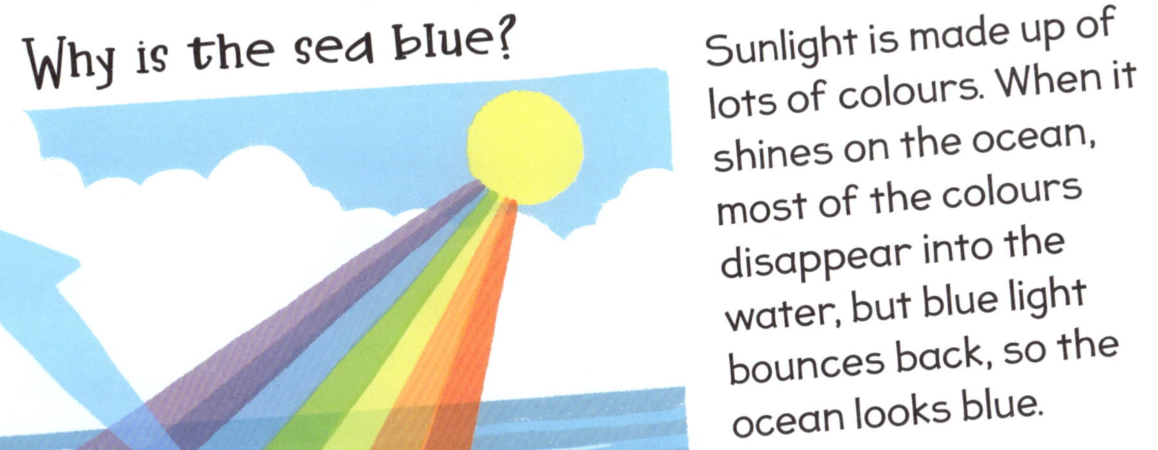

Sunlight is made up of lots of colours. When it shines on the ocean, most of the colours disappear into the water, but blue light bounces back, so the ocean looks blue.

What is a fish?

Fish are animals that have skeletons, gills and fins. There are more than 32,000 types, and most of them live in oceans.

Tail fin swishes from side to side when swimming

Overlapping scales are smooth and slippery

Herring

I'm the perfect shape for swimming. My silvery scales help water to flow easily over my skin.

Slim, sleek body moves quickly through water

Can people breathe underwater too?

No – sorry! You need to breathe air because you have lungs. All fish have special organs called gills that work in water.

Water and air have oxygen gas in them. All animals need oxygen to live.

Oxygen-rich water flows in

Triggerfish

Water flows out over the gills, where the oxygen passes into the fish's blood

Do fish have special homes?

Some do. Clownfish live among the tentacles of stinging sea anemones. The fish are covered in special slime that protects them from stings, but animals that might want to eat them can't get close!

Can fish fly?

No – but some can glide. Flying fish have very streamlined bodies and use their big fins to launch out of the water into the air.

How is my nose like a shark?

Did you know?

At 3 metres long, the ocean **sunfish** is one of the world's biggest bony fish.

A **hairy frogfish** is a fast eater. It sucks food into its mouth like a vacuum cleaner – 50 times faster than the blink of an eye!

Octopuses can turn red when they are angry.

Electric rays can zap fish with an electric shock. Once the fish has been stunned, the ray can eat it!

Seaweed is often used as a thickener in ice cream!

The **sperm whale** has the biggest brain on the planet – and probably the whole Universe!

500 million years ago the only living things on Earth were in the ocean.

Baby sharks and baby seals are called **pups**, and baby fish are called **fry**.

Shark skin feels like sandpaper. It is covered in tiny bumpy scales that help them slip through the water.

Whales and **dolphins** aren't fish – they are mammals.

A **great white shark** can eat enough meat to make 3000 burgers in one go, and it won't want to eat again for at least ten days.

Polar bears and **penguins** never meet because penguins live near the South Pole and polar bears live near the North Pole!

Sailors used to think that **dugongs** were mermaids. They're actually plump mammals that spend their time grazing on sea plants.

Do trees grow in the deep sea?

No – but giant kelp seaweed grows in huge forests! It is found in the Pacific Ocean, and can grow up to 50 centimetres in one day.

Who picnics at the bottom of the sea?

Marine iguanas do! They dive to depths of 12 metres – and stay there for up to an hour while they nibble on seaweed that grows on the seabed.

Do baby fish go to nursery?

Young fish and reptiles keep away from predators in special hiding places called nurseries. Shallow waters around sea grasses and mangrove tree roots make good nurseries.

What do turtles eat?

Green sea turtles feast on fields of sea grasses that grow underwater.

Who plays hide and seek?

Many ocean animals do! On coral reefs, millions of sea creatures live close together. Lots of them use clever tricks to avoid being eaten by the others.

Do fish need friends?

Can you see a reef from space?

Yes! The Great Barrier Reef stretches over 2000 kilometres off the coast of Australia. Reefs are built by tiny animals called polyps. Each one lives in its own rocky cup, waving its tentacles in the water.

How long does it take to make an island?

If a volcano erupts on the seabed, it can make an island in a few years! Lava (a type of liquid rock) pours out and builds up to create a brand new island.

Volcano erupts on seabed

A cone shape of lava forms on the seabed

The cone grows so big it breaks the surface – it's a new island!

Can I find treasure on an island?

Yes – but not the sort that belongs to pirates! The treasure to be found on islands is all the precious animals that live on them.

Who lives on an island?

Islands are often home to animals that live nowhere else on Earth. About 60 types of lemur live only on the island of Madagascar, which is in the Indian Ocean.

How many?

About 100 million sharks are killed by people every year.

400 million

The number of years that sharks have lived in the oceans.

There are more volcanoes under the sea than on land! **452** are on the edges of the Pacific Ocean.

Pufferfish have poisonous flesh. About **30** people die every year after eating them.

7 metres

The length of the biggest saltwater crocodiles.

A starfish can have more than **30** arms!

There were **40 million** crabs on Christmas Island – until yellow crazy ants arrived. They spray the crabs with acid and eat them, so far killing about **15 million** of them.

40,000

...the number of eggs a herring can lay in one go.

507

...the incredible age in years of a clam that was found in the Atlantic Ocean.

Phew!

A narwhal's giant tooth can reach **3 metres** in length.

350

The number of types of coral that live in the Great Barrier Reef.

1 million seabirds are killed every year by plastic rubbish that is in the ocean.

Who sleeps in a muddy bed?

Sea cucumbers do! These slug-like animals live in mud, eat mud and poo mud! Sea cucumbers are animals, not vegetables, but some people do like to eat them!

How do people explore under the sea?

People can't breathe in water, but we still find ways to explore the deep ocean. We can scuba dive, use submarines, or send robots with cameras.

Remotely operated underwater vehicles are one way for people to explore deep water from the safety of the surface

Who stands on three legs?

Tripod fish have three long, leg-like fins to stand on the seabed. Each fin-leg can be more than 50 centimetres long! Then they keep their mouths open and wait for food to swim right in.

Who lights up the deep, dark sea?

Sunlight can't reach the bottom of the deep sea. So some animals make their own light instead!

Viperfish like me use flashing lights to attract little animals to swim close. Then we swallow them up! My mouth is so big I can swallow animals bigger than me!

Why does the sea go in and out?

Over the course of a day at the seaside you will see the sea moving in and out. This is called the tide, and it's caused by the Moon!

Why is there jelly in a rock pool?

Who loves to surf?

Humans – but dolphins ride the waves too! Flat water turns to waves when wind blows over the top of it.

Which animals go to school?

Who snacks at the shore?

Grey seals feed on all kinds of animals near the shore, from crabs to seabirds. They can also dive to depths of 70 metres when hunting.

Would you rather?

Which would you prefer – soaring with a **sea eagle** or surfing with a **penguin**?

Would you rather be covered in spikes like a **pineapplefish** or have a huge mouth like a **jawfish**?

Would you rather be a **marine biologist** and study ocean animals, or a **marine geologist** and find out all about the mysterious seabed?

Would it be nicer to hold hands with a furry **sea otter**...

... or with a **blind hairy yeti crab**?

Is it better to have your feet nibbled by a **cleaner fish**, or tickled by a **feather duster worm**?

Would you rather have teeth as big as a **walrus's tusks**, or a long nose like a **sailfish**?

i'm the size of an elephant and consume 200 litres of milk a day!

Would you like to eat as much as a **baby blue whale**...

...or as little as a **mother octopus**?

i don't eat anything while i look after my eggs – and that can take eight months!

Who walks on water?

Polar bears do. They live in the Arctic Ocean. It's so cold there that the ocean freezes over.

Why don't fish freeze?

Icefish have special blood that doesn't freeze – even if the water around them turns to ice!

Why do icebergs float?

Icebergs are made of frozen water. Ice is lighter than water, so it floats. Big sheets of ice float on the sea too. They are good places for penguins and seals to take a nap when they are tired of swimming, slipping and sliding!

Who packs a powerful punch?

A peacock mantis shrimp is one of the world's strongest animals for its size! It uses its club-like legs to wallop other animals at lightning speed.

Which fish has the most vicious venom?

Why do jellyfish sting?

A jellyfish uses its long, stinging tentacles to get a meal. Each tentacle carries tiny, venomous darts that jab passing fish prey.

Who can smell a drop of blood in the sea?

Sharks can! These incredible hunters have a super sense of smell that helps them find fish and other animals to eat.

Are there monsters in the sea?

There are some very big animals in the sea... but no monsters. From huge rays and outsize crabs to the biggest animal on Earth – plenty of giants lurk in the deep.

That's how they breathe! Whales breathe air. They all have one or two blowholes, which are like nostrils. A spout from a whale is really just a big, warm, wet breath!

Which crab has the longest legs?

A Japanese spider crab has 10 legs, and each leg can be over 2 metres long! These mega crabs can reach 100 years old.

Could you sink a ship?
Giant manta ray
No! Sailors used to think fish like me could pull a ship under the water. They even called me devil fish! It wasn't true – I'm huge (up to 7 metres wide) but harmless.
Giant octopus
Blue whale
Who can reach you from 4 metres away?
Me! My eight arms are each 4 metres long, with more than 200 strong suckers on each one.

A compendium of questions

Can I drink seawater?

No – it can make you sick. Seawater is too salty, and often dirty too. The dirt is called pollution and it's bad for all living things.

Can I swim across an ocean?

No human has ever swum across one without taking a break in a boat. But whales, sharks and turtles can!

Why do thresher sharks have such long tails?

They use the enormous upper lobes of their tail fins to wallop shoals of their fish prey.

Which fish ties itself in knots?

A hagfish! It's covered in slippery slime and ties itself in knots when it is feasting on dead animals at the bottom of the sea.

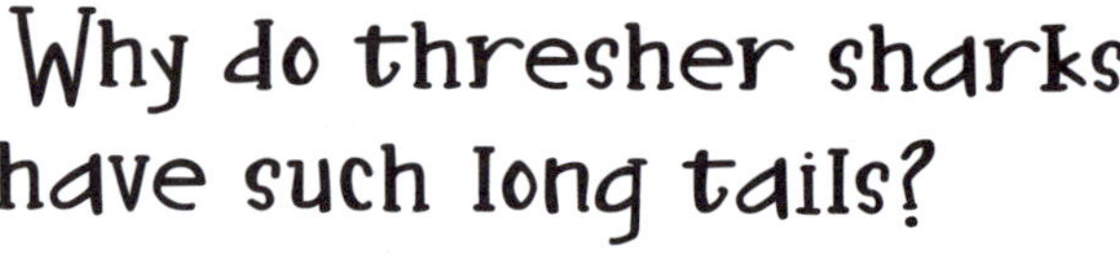

An octopus can work out how to open a jar to reach food inside! It uses its suckers to grip shellfish and rip them open.

Why is a blobfish so ugly?

When a blobfish is brought to the surface of the sea its soft, spongy flesh goes floppy. When it is busy hunting in the deep sea it looks quite different.

Why does a firefly squid glow?

To hide, and to be seen! This squid can mimic the light above or below it if it wants to hide, and glow brightly when it wants to attract a mate.

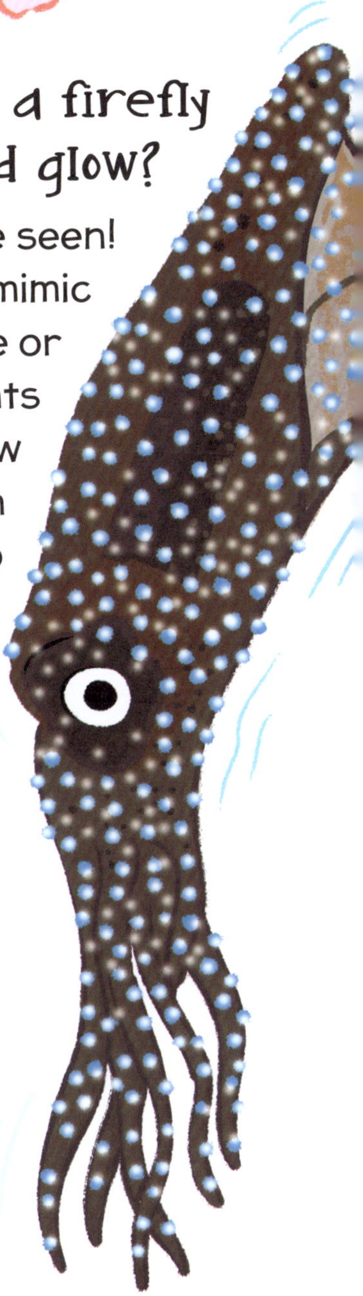

Did that fish's eye just move?

Maybe! Baby flounders have an eye on each side of their head. As they grow, one eye moves to join the other – so the adult flounder can spend its days lying on the seafloor.

Which fish uses oars?

The fins of the strange, ribbon-like oarfish look a bit like oars. It's the longest bony fish – reaching up to 11 metres.